This book

If you find this book, please return

it to the following address:

_____

_____

_____

or call or text:

_____

or email:

_____

Read Through

The Bible

in a Year

Journal

By

Rob Westbrook

My Read Through The Bible in a Year Journal

by Rob Westbrook

You're in for the Adventure of Your Life!

Welcome! You are about to set out on a wonderful and epic adventure! Your choice to read through the Bible this year may well be one of the greatest and most life-changing choices you have ever made. Millions and millions of lives have already been changed by the living Word of God, the Bible. And yours could be next!

Here's what the Bible says about itself: "For the word of God is living and active, sharper than any two-edged sword, piercing to the division of soul and spirit, of joints and marrow, and discerning the thoughts and intentions of the heart" (Hebrews 4:12 ESV). This year God will use His word to show Himself to you in totally new ways. And He will reveal and change your heart in the process.

There's no better way to hear from God than through His word. You will hear His voice from the pristine Garden of Eden, from the solemn hill called Golgotha, and from the windswept barren island of Patmos. His voice will whisper to you from the wastelands of the Exodus wilderness. And He will shout "It is finished!" to you from a cruel Roman cross.

Get ready for the ride of your life! God is speaking. And He is about to speak to you!

Getting Started

Of course, the first item needed in your quest is a Bible. There are many, many translations available, in all forms. There's reference Bibles, study Bibles, and devotional bibles. With the technology of today, there's also online Bibles, eReader Bibles, and Bible apps. Any of these Bibles will be fine for you as you read through the Bible this year. The key here is to choose one form and use it consistently throughout the year. Choosing one form for the entire year helps you keep everything in one place. You'll be better able to return to previous readings if you stick to one form. So make your choice now. Are you going with a print Bible? Are you going to use a particular app on your phone? Select a form and settle that decision now.

I will be using this form of the Bible to read this year:

_____

The next choice to make is a Bible translation. There are also many, many Bible translations available today. You can go with the rich, poetic prose of the King James Version, or you can decide to go with The Message paraphrase. Or you can choose from the many translations between them. The important factor here is reading and comprehension. Select a translation you are comfortable reading and you can understand. So what version are you going to use this year?

I will be using this translation as I read through the Bible this year:

_____

Once you've settled on a translation, decide when and where you will do your daily reading. Consistency is important. Reading the Bible every day needs to become a habit. Building this consistent habit is made simpler when you have a certain location and time to do your reading. Of course, there will be times when you will not be able to be at this certain place or able to read at this certain time. But you should establish a place and time anyway. The more consistent you are with your reading time and place, the easier it becomes to follow through. You may choose your favorite recliner, porch swing, or Starbucks as your location. If you're a morning person, you may read at 6:00 am every day. Or you may read on your lunch break at noon. Whatever works best for you, make the place and time a habit. Consistency is the key to completing your goal of reading through the Bible this year.

I will do my daily Bible reading at the following location:

_____

I will do my daily Bible reading every day at the following time:

_____

There are going to be days when you don't get to do your daily Bible reading. There may be a period of days when you miss your reading. It happens to everyone. Don't panic. Don't give up. When you get back to your reading, just pick up where you left off. If you've missed one day, read both days. If you've missed more than one day, split the reading up so that you can be back on schedule within a week. For instance, say you've missed three days of reading. Start where you last read, and read two days of reading for the next three days. That will put you back on schedule. The important key here is to never get frustrated with yourself and quit altogether. Stuff happens. It happens to us all. Get back to it as soon as possible.

How to Use This Journal

Each page of this journal is dedicated to one day of your Bible reading. The page is divided into four sections.

The first section, at the top of the page, gives you the **Bible passage** to read for that day. The passages are arranged so that in 365 days, you will entirely read the Bible. There's a check box below the passage listing and a line to enter the date of your reading. When you finish your reading check that box and enter the date. It seems trivial to check a box and record a date, but there's something about finishing your reading and checking it off the list. Make sure you always do this.

The next section on the page is a **Notes** section. As you read, you'll find yourself wanting to remember things you've read. The reading may raise some questions you have. The Notes section is there for you to record those items. As you do your reading, have your journal nearby with a pen, and jot those items down as they occur to you. This gives you a way to remember those items before they fade away. Later, you can refer back to your notes to think more about what you've read or to remember the questions you have. Use the Notes section judiciously.

Below the Notes section there's a section with the heading **What God is Saying to Me**. As you read, you will sometimes sense God is speaking directly to you through the Bible passage. Record those impressions in this section. You now have a reference to what God is saying to you. One of the pleasures of keeping a journal is going back weeks, months, or even years later, and seeing how God was speaking and leading you at that time. Use this section. You'll be thankful you did.

The last section is the **Prayer** section. Every day, you should begin with a prayer. Ask God to show you everything He wants you to see. Ask Him for clarity and understanding. But you should also pray when you finish the daily reading. You've just spent time with God and He's working in you to make you more like Jesus. Write out a prayer in this section, putting on paper what you are saying in your heart. Add personal prayer requests here, as well. Bible reading and prayer go hand in hand. God speaks to you through His word and you speak back to Him in prayer. Don't miss out on this time with the Lord.

As you read, you'll find little hints and reminders at the bottom of the page giving you an indication of your progress. You'll see how many days it will take to complete a book and how far you've traveled through the year. These help you see you are making progress toward your goal of reading the Bible in a year.

Examples are always helpful. Take a look at the next page to see an example of one day's reading in the journal.

Day 337: Ephesians 1 - 3

| ☒ | I read this passage on | 10 | / | 01 | / 2012 |

Prayer	Notes
Father, thank you for	I once was dead in my sins but, through Jesus, I'm
my salvation! Thank	now alive. Because of God's mercy and grace I am
you that you've done it	saved! God now wants me to do the good things He's
all for me in Jesus!	had planned for me since time began.
Now give me your	**What God is saying to me**
guidance to the plans	My salvation is complete in Jesus. I don't have to
you've got for me now.	impress Him, just trust Him. He has a plan for my
Amen.	life and it begins now!

Congratulations again on your choice to read through the Bible this year. Jump in with enthusiasm. Don't get discouraged. And don't quit. God has something to say to you this year and you don't want to miss it!

Day 1: Genesis 1 - 3

❏ I read this passage on / /	
Prayer	**Notes**
_____	
_____	_____
_____	_____
_____	_____
_____	_____
_____	**What God is saying to me**
_____	_____
_____	_____
_____	_____
_____	_____

You've just took a huge step in completing your goal – you started!

In just **16 days** you'll finish the book of Genesis. 364 days until you're finished.

Day 2: Genesis 4 - 6

☐ I read this passage on / /

Prayer	Notes
	What God is saying to me

Day 3: Genesis 7 - 9

❑ I read this passage on / /

Prayer	Notes
_____	
	_____
_____	
	_____
_____	
	_____
_____	
_____	**What God is saying to me**
	_____
_____	
	_____
_____	
	_____
_____	
	_____
_____	

Day 4: Genesis 10 - 12

❏ I read this passage on / /

Prayer	Notes
_____	_____
_____	_____
_____	_____
_____	_____
_____	**What God is saying to me**
_____	_____
_____	_____
_____	_____
_____	_____

Day 5: Genesis 13 - 15

❏ I read this passage on / /	

Prayer	Notes
_____	_____
_____	_____
_____	_____
_____	_____
_____	**What God is saying to me**
_____	_____
_____	_____
_____	_____
_____	_____

Day 6: Genesis 16 - 18

❏ I read this passage on	/	/

Prayer	Notes

What God is saying to me

Day 7: Genesis 19 - 21

❏ I read this passage on / /

Prayer	Notes
	What God is saying to me

Day 8: Genesis 22 - 24

	❑ I read this passage on / /
Prayer	**Notes**
_____	
	_____
_____	
	_____
_____	
	_____
_____	
	_____
_____	**What God is saying to me**
_____	_____
_____	_____
_____	_____
_____	_____

You're halfway through Genesis already!

357 days until you're finished.

Day 9: Genesis 25 - 27

☐ I read this passage on / /	
Prayer	**Notes**
_____	_____
_____	_____
_____	_____
_____	_____
_____	**What God is saying to me**
_____	_____
_____	_____
_____	_____
_____	_____
_____	_____

Day 10: Genesis 28 - 30

❑ I read this passage on / /

Prayer	Notes
_____	
	_____
_____	
	_____
_____	
	_____
_____	
	_____
_____	**What God is saying to me**
_____	_____
_____	_____
_____	_____
_____	_____
_____	_____

Day 11: Genesis 31 - 33

	I read this passage on / /

Prayer	Notes

What God is saying to me

Day 12: Genesis 34 - 36

❏ I read this passage on / /	
Prayer	**Notes**
	What God is saying to me

Day 13: Genesis 37 - 39

❑ I read this passage on / /	
Prayer	**Notes**
	What God is saying to me

Day 14: Genesis 40 - 42

☐ I read this passage on	/	/
Prayer	**Notes**	

What God is saying to me

Day 15: Genesis 43 - 46

| ❑ I read this passage on | / | / |

Prayer	Notes

What God is saying to me

24

Day 16: Genesis 47 - 50

| ❑ | I read this passage on | / | / |

Prayer	Notes
	What God is saying to me

You've just finished Genesis! See there, it wasn't that hard. That's **1 of 66** books complete.

349 days until you're finished.

Day 17: Exodus 1 - 3

	☐ I read this passage on / /
Prayer	**Notes**

What God is saying to me

Exodus is a shorter book than Genesis. It will take you only **13 days** to finish.

348 days until you're finished.

Day 18: Exodus 4 - 6

☐ I read this passage on   /   /

Prayer	Notes
	What God is saying to me

Day 19: Exodus 7 - 9

Prayer	Notes
☐ I read this passage on / /	

Prayer	Notes

What God is saying to me

Day 20: Exodus 10 - 12

	❑ I read this passage on / /
Prayer	**Notes**

What God is saying to me

Day 21: Exodus 13 - 15

❏	I read this passage on / /
Prayer	**Notes**

What God is saying to me

Day 22: Exodus 16 - 18

❏   I read this passage on   /   /

Prayer	Notes

What God is saying to me

Day 23: Exodus 19 - 21

❑ I read this passage on / /	
Prayer	**Notes**
	What God is saying to me

You're halfway through Exodus. You're making progress!

342 days until you're finished.

Day 24: Exodus 22 - 24

❑ I read this passage on	/	/

Prayer	Notes
_____	
	_____
_____	
	_____
_____	
	_____
_____	
	_____
_____	**What God is saying to me**
_____	_____
_____	_____
_____	_____
_____	_____
	_____

Day 25: Exodus 25 - 27

Prayer	Notes

What God is saying to me

Day 26: Exodus 28 - 30

❏ I read this passage on / /	
Prayer	**Notes**
	What God is saying to me

Day 27: Exodus 31 - 33

❑ I read this passage on / /	

Prayer	Notes
	What God is saying to me

Day 28: Exodus 34 - 36

❏ I read this passage on / /

Prayer	Notes
_____	
	_____
_____	
	_____
_____	
	_____
_____	
	_____
_____	**What God is saying to me**
_____	_____
_____	_____
_____	_____
_____	_____
	_____

Day 29: Exodus 37 - 40

❑ I read this passage on / /	

Prayer	Notes
_____	_____
_____	_____
_____	_____
_____	_____
_____	**What God is saying to me**
_____	_____
_____	_____
_____	_____
_____	_____

And you're done with Exodus! Keep pushing ahead. That's **2 of 66** books complete.

336 days until you're finished.

Day 30: Leviticus 1 - 3

❏ I read this passage on	/	/

Prayer	Notes
_____	_____
_____	_____
_____	_____
_____	_____
_____	**What God is saying to me**
_____	_____
_____	_____
_____	_____
_____	_____

In only **9 days** you'll finish Leviticus and 3 books of the Bible!

335 days until you're finished.

Day 31: Leviticus 4 - 6

❏	I read this passage on / /
Prayer	**Notes**
	What God is saying to me

Day 32: Leviticus 7 - 9

❏ I read this passage on / /

Prayer	Notes
	What God is saying to me

Day 33: Leviticus 10 - 12

	❏ I read this passage on / /
Prayer	**Notes**

What God is saying to me

Day 34: Leviticus 13 - 15

Prayer	Notes
❑ I read this passage on / /	

Prayer | **Notes**

_____

_____

_____

_____

_____

What God is saying to me

_____

_____

_____

_____

You're at the halfway mark of reading Leviticus. Good progress!

331 days until you're finished.

Day 35: Leviticus 16 - 18

❏ I read this passage on	/	/

Prayer	Notes
_____	_____
_____	_____
_____	_____
_____	_____
_____	**What God is saying to me**
_____	_____
_____	_____
_____	_____
_____	_____

Day 36: Leviticus 19 - 21

❏ I read this passage on	/	/

Prayer	Notes

What God is saying to me

Day 37: Leviticus 22 - 24

❏ I read this passage on	/	/

Prayer	Notes

What God is saying to me

You have now read **10%** of the Bible. That's progress!

328 days until you're finished.

Day 38: Leviticus 25 - 27

❑   I read this passage on   /   /

Prayer	Notes

What God is saying to me

That completes your reading through Leviticus! That's **3 of 66** books complete.

327 days until you're finished.

Day 39: Numbers 1 - 3

❏ I read this passage on / /	
Prayer	**Notes**
_____	_____
_____	_____
_____	_____
_____	_____
_____	**What God is saying to me**
_____	_____
_____	_____
_____	_____
_____	_____

It will take you **12 days** to read through the book of Numbers.

326 days until you're finished.

Day 40: Numbers 4 - 6

❑ I read this passage on / /	
Prayer	**Notes**

What God is saying to me

Day 41: Numbers 7 - 9

	❏ I read this passage on / /
Prayer	**Notes**

What God is saying to me

Day 42: Numbers 10 - 12

❑ I read this passage on   /   /

Prayer	Notes

What God is saying to me

Day 43: Numbers 13 - 15

| ❑ I read this passage on   /   / |

Prayer	Notes

What God is saying to me

Day 44: Numbers 16 - 18

❑ I read this passage on / /

Prayer	Notes
_____	
	_____
_____	
	_____
_____	
	_____
_____	
	_____
_____	**What God is saying to me**
	_____
_____	
	_____
_____	
	_____
_____	
	_____
_____	

You're halfway through Numbers.

321 days until you're finished.

Day 45: Numbers 19 - 21

❑   I read this passage on   /   /

Prayer	Notes

What God is saying to me

Day 46: Numbers 22 - 24

❑ I read this passage on / /

Prayer	Notes
	What God is saying to me

Day 47: Numbers 25 - 27

❏ I read this passage on / /

Prayer	Notes
	What God is saying to me

Day 48: Numbers 28 - 30

❑ I read this passage on	/	/

Prayer	Notes

What God is saying to me

Day 49: Numbers 31 - 33

| | ❑ I read this passage on | / | / |

Prayer

Notes

What God is saying to me

Day 50: Numbers 34 - 36

☐ I read this passage on	/	/

Prayer	Notes

What God is saying to me

You've finished the book of Numbers. You are making great progress. That's **4 of 66** books complete.
315 days until you're finished.

Day 51: Deuteronomy 1 - 3

☐ I read this passage on   /   /

Prayer	Notes

What God is saying to me

It will take **11 days** to read through Deuteronomy.

314 days until you're finished.

Day 52: Deuteronomy 4 - 6

❑ I read this passage on	/	/

Prayer	Notes

What God is saying to me

Day 53: Deuteronomy 7 - 9

❑   I read this passage on   /   /

Prayer	Notes

What God is saying to me

Day 54: Deuteronomy 10 - 12

❏   I read this passage on   /   /

Prayer	Notes

What God is saying to me

Day 55: Deuteronomy 13 - 15

❑ I read this passage on	/	/

Prayer	Notes
_____	
_____	_____
_____	_____
_____	_____
_____	_____
_____	**What God is saying to me**
_____	_____
_____	_____
_____	_____
_____	_____
_____	_____

Day 56: Deuteronomy 16 - 18

❑ I read this passage on / /	
Prayer	**Notes**
	What God is saying to me

This is the halfway mark through the book of Deuteronomy.

309 days until you're finished.

Day 57: Deuteronomy 19 - 21

❑ I read this passage on   /   /

Prayer	Notes

What God is saying to me

Day 58: Deuteronomy 22 - 24

❏ I read this passage on	/ /

Prayer	Notes
_____	_____
	_____
_____	_____
	_____
_____	_____
	_____
_____	
	What God is saying to me
_____	_____
	_____
_____	_____
	_____
_____	_____
	_____
_____	_____

Day 59: Deuteronomy 25 - 27

	❏ I read this passage on / /
Prayer	**Notes**
	What God is saying to me

Day 60: Deuteronomy 28 - 30

❏ I read this passage on / /	
Prayer	Notes
_____ _____ _____ _____ _____	_____ _____ _____ _____
	What God is saying to me
_____ _____ _____ _____	_____ _____ _____ _____

Day 61: Deuteronomy 31 - 34

❏ I read this passage on / /	

Prayer	Notes
	What God is saying to me

You've finished Deuteronomy and what the Hebrews call the Torah. That's **5 of 66** books complete.

304 days until you're finished.

Day 62: Joshua 1 - 3

	I read this passage on 01 / 01 / 2019

Prayer	Notes
That I would be fed by the Word & commit myself to reading the bible this year so that it would be life giving & nurturing. Lord, may I come & feast at your table.	Rahab is the heroine. Showed faith & was redeemed even despite her past.

What God is saying to me

Parting the Jordan River → men had to take the first step in faith before God revealed Himself through a miracle.

It will take **8 days** to read through Joshua.

303 days until you're finished.

Day 63: Joshua 4 - 6

	I read this passage on 01 / 02 / 19
Prayer	Notes

Notes

Faith in obeying God.

(Are the twelve stones still there?)

Rahab is spared.

What God is saying to me

Day 64: Joshua 7 - 9

☐ I read this passage on	/	/

Prayer	Notes

What God is saying to me

Day 65: Joshua 10 - 12

❏   I read this passage on   /   /

Prayer	Notes

What God is saying to me

Already halfway through Joshua.

300 days until you're finished.

Day 66: Joshua 13 - 15

| ☐ I read this passage on | / | / |

Prayer	Notes
	What God is saying to me

299 days until you're finished.

Day 67: Joshua 16 - 18

Prayer	Notes

❏ I read this passage on   /   /

What God is saying to me

Day 68: Joshua 19 - 21

❏   I read this passage on   /   /

Prayer	Notes

What God is saying to me

Day 69: Joshua 22 -24

	❑ I read this passage on / /
Prayer	**Notes**
_____	
	_____
_____	
	_____
_____	
	_____
_____	
	_____
_____	**What God is saying to me**
_____	_____
_____	_____
_____	_____
_____	_____

And that finishes Joshua! That's **6 of 66** books complete.

296 days until you're finished.

Day 70: Judges 1 - 3

☐ I read this passage on	/	/

Prayer	Notes
_____	
	_____
_____	
	_____
_____	
	_____
_____	
	What God is saying to me
_____	
	_____
_____	
	_____
_____	
	_____
_____	
	_____
_____	

It will take you **7 days** to read through Judges.

295 days until you're finished.

Day 71: Judges 4 - 6

❑ I read this passage on / /	
Prayer	**Notes**
	What God is saying to me

Day 72: Judges 7 - 9

❑ I read this passage on / /	
Prayer	**Notes**

What God is saying to me

Today marks your <u>20%</u> complete mark in reading through the Bible.

293 days until you're finished.

Day 73: Judges 10 - 12

Prayer	Notes
	What God is saying to me

You're over halfway through Judges.

292 days until you're finished.

Day 74: Judges 13 - 15

❑ I read this passage on   /   /

Prayer	Notes

What God is saying to me

Day 75: Judges 16 - 18

❑ I read this passage on / /	
Prayer	**Notes**
_____	_____
_____	_____
_____	_____
_____	_____
_____	**What God is saying to me**
_____	_____
_____	_____
_____	_____
_____	_____

84

Day 76: Judges 19 - 21

❏   I read this passage on   /   /

Prayer	Notes
_____	
	_____
_____	
	_____
_____	
	_____
_____	
	_____
_____	**What God is saying to me**
_____	_____
_____	_____
_____	_____
_____	_____
_____	_____

Judges is in the book. You've finished it. That's **7 of 66** books complete.

289 days until you're finished.

Day 77: Ruth 1 - 4

	I read this passage on　　　/　　　/
Prayer	**Notes**

What God is saying to me

You've read the whole book of Ruth at one sitting. That's quick! That's **8 of 66** books complete.
288 days until you're finished.

Day 78: 1 Samuel 1 - 3

❑ I read this passage on	/	/

Prayer	Notes
	What God is saying to me

It will take **10 days** to read through 1 Samuel.

287 days until you're finished.

Day 79: 1 Samuel 4 - 6

❏ I read this passage on / /

Prayer	Notes
	What God is saying to me

286 days until you're finished.

Day 80: 1 Samuel 7 - 9

❑ I read this passage on / /

Prayer	Notes
_____	_____
	_____
_____	_____
	_____
_____	
_____	
	What God is saying to me
_____	_____
_____	_____
_____	_____
_____	_____
_____	_____

Day 81: 1 Samuel 10 - 12

❏ I read this passage on / /	
Prayer	**Notes**
	What God is saying to me

Day 82: 1 Samuel 13 - 15

	I read this passage on / /

Prayer	Notes

What God is saying to me

Halfway done with 1 Samuel.
283 days until you're finished.

Day 83: 1 Samuel 16 - 18

❏ I read this passage on   /   /

Prayer	Notes

What God is saying to me

Day 84: 1 Samuel 19 - 21

| ☐ I read this passage on | / | / |

Prayer	Notes
	What God is saying to me

Day 85: 1 Samuel 22 - 24

❑ I read this passage on   /   /

Prayer	Notes

What God is saying to me

Day 86: 1 Samuel 25 - 27

❏ I read this passage on / /	
Prayer	**Notes**
	What God is saying to me

Day 87: 1 Samuel 28 - 31

❑	I read this passage on	/ /

Prayer	Notes

What God is saying to me

That completes 1 Samuel. Tomorrow you start 2 Samuel. That's **9 of 66** books complete.

278 days until you're finished.

Day 88: 2 Samuel 1 - 3

☐ I read this passage on   /   /

Prayer	Notes
_____	_____
	_____
_____	_____
_____	_____
_____	
	What God is saying to me
_____	_____
_____	_____
_____	_____
_____	_____
_____	_____

It will take you **8 days** to read through 2 Samuel.

277 days until you're finished.

Day 89: 2 Samuel 4 - 6

❏ I read this passage on	/	/

Prayer	Notes
	What God is saying to me

Day 90: 2 Samuel 7 - 9

❑   I read this passage on   /   /

Prayer	Notes
	What God is saying to me

Day 91: 2 Samuel 10 - 12

❑ I read this passage on / /	
Prayer	**Notes**
	What God is saying to me

Halfway through 2 Samuel already!

274 days until you're finished.

Day 92: 2 Samuel 13 - 15

❏ I read this passage on	/	/

Prayer	Notes
_____	
	_____
_____	
	_____
_____	
	_____
_____	
	_____
_____	**What God is saying to me**
_____	_____
_____	_____
_____	_____
_____	_____

Good job! You are already __25%__ complete in your journey through the Word of God.

273 days until you're finished.

Day 93: 2 Samuel 16 - 18

Prayer	❑ I read this passage on / /
	Notes
	What God is saying to me

Day 94: 2 Samuel 19 - 21

Prayer	Notes
❑ I read this passage on / /	

What God is saying to me

Day 95: 2 Samuel 22 - 24

Prayer	Notes

What God is saying to me

You've finished 2 Samuel. That's **10 of 66** books complete.

270 days until you're finished.

Day 96: 1 Kings 1 - 3

❏ I read this passage on   /   /

Prayer	Notes
_____	
	_____
_____	
	_____
_____	
	_____
_____	
	_____
_____	**What God is saying to me**
_____	_____
_____	_____
_____	_____
_____	_____
_____	_____

It will take **7 days** to read through 1 Kings.

269 days until you're finished.

Day 97: 1 Kings 4 - 6

❏   I read this passage on   /   /

Prayer	Notes

What God is saying to me

Day 98: 1 Kings 7 - 9

	I read this passage on / /

Prayer	Notes
	What God is saying to me

Day 99: 1 Kings 10 - 12

❏ I read this passage on / /

Prayer	Notes

What God is saying to me

You've reached the halfway mark of 1 Kings.

266 days until you're finished.

Day 100: 1 Kings 13 - 15

❏ I read this passage on / /	
Prayer	**Notes**
	What God is saying to me

Day 101: 1 Kings 16 - 18

❏ I read this passage on	/	/

Prayer	Notes

What God is saying to me

Day 102: 1 Kings 19 - 22

| | ❏ I read this passage on | / | / |

Prayer	Notes

What God is saying to me

Good progress. You're already finished with 1 Kings. That's **11 of 66** books complete.

263 days until you're finished.

Day 103: 2 Kings 1 - 3

❏ I read this passage on   /   /

Prayer	Notes

What God is saying to me

It will take **8 days** to finish reading 2 Kings.

262 days until you're finished.

Day 104: 2 Kings 4 - 6

☐ I read this passage on / /

Prayer	Notes
	What God is saying to me

Day 105: 2 Kings 7 - 9

❑ I read this passage on	/	/

Prayer	Notes

What God is saying to me

Day 106: 2 Kings 10 - 12

	❏ I read this passage on / /
Prayer	**Notes**
_____	
	_____
_____	
	_____
_____	
	_____
_____	
	_____
_____	**What God is saying to me**
_____	_____
_____	_____
_____	_____
_____	_____

You're halfway through 2 Kings.

259 days until you're finished.

Day 107: 2 Kings 13 - 15

❑   I read this passage on   /   /

Prayer	Notes

What God is saying to me

Day 108: 2 Kings 16 - 18

❏ I read this passage on / /	

Prayer	Notes
	What God is saying to me

Day 109: 2 Kings 19 - 21

❏ I read this passage on / /

Prayer	Notes

What God is saying to me

Day 110: 2 Kings 22 - 25

❏ I read this passage on	/	/

Prayer	Notes

What God is saying to me

You've now read **30%** of the Bible!

You've finished the book of 2 Kings. That's **12 of 66** books complete. 255 days until you're finished.

Day 111: 1 Chronicles 1 - 6

❏ I read this passage on   /   /

Prayer	Notes

What God is saying to me

It will take **8 days** to read through 1 Chronicles.

254 days until you're finished.

Day 112: 1 Chronicles 7 - 9

❑ I read this passage on	/ /

Prayer	Notes
_____	_____
_____	_____
_____	_____
_____	_____
	_____
_____	**What God is saying to me**
_____	_____
_____	_____
_____	_____
_____	_____

Day 113: 1 Chronicles 10 - 12

❏ I read this passage on	/	/

Prayer	Notes

What God is saying to me

Day 114: 1 Chronicles 13 - 15

❏ I read this passage on	/ /

Prayer	Notes
_____	
	_____
_____	
	_____
_____	
	_____
_____	
	_____
_____	**What God is saying to me**
_____	_____
_____	_____
_____	_____
_____	_____

Day 115: 1 Chronicles 16 - 18

	I read this passage on / /
Prayer	**Notes**

What God is saying to me

Day 116: 1 Chronicles 19 - 21

	I read this passage on	/	/

Prayer	Notes
	What God is saying to me

Day 117: 1 Chronicles 22 - 25

❏ I read this passage on / /

Prayer	Notes
	What God is saying to me

Day 118: 1 Chronicles 26 - 29

☐ I read this passage on / /

Prayer	Notes
_____	_____
	_____
_____	_____
	_____
_____	_____
	_____
_____	**What God is saying to me**
	_____
_____	_____
	_____
_____	_____
	_____
_____	_____
	_____
_____	_____

You've just finished 1 Chronicles. That's **13 of 66** books complete.

247 days until you're finished.

Day 119: 2 Chronicles 1 - 3

❏	I read this passage on	/	/

Prayer	Notes

What God is saying to me

It will take **12 days** to read the book of 2 Chronicles.

246 days until you're finished.

Day 120: 2 Chronicles 4 - 6

❏ I read this passage on / /	
Prayer	**Notes**
	What God is saying to me

Day 121: 2 Chronicles 7 - 9

❑ I read this passage on	/	/

Prayer	Notes

What God is saying to me

Day 122: 2 Chronicles 10 - 12

❏ I read this passage on   /   /

Prayer	Notes

What God is saying to me

Day 123: 2 Chronicles 13 - 15

❏   I read this passage on   /   /

Prayer	Notes

What God is saying to me

Day 124: 2 Chronicles 16 - 18

| ❏ I read this passage on | / | / |

Prayer	Notes

What God is saying to me

This is the halfway mark of 2 Chronicles.

241 days until you're finished.

Day 125: 2 Chronicles 19 - 21

❏ I read this passage on / /	
Prayer	**Notes**
	What God is saying to me

Day 126: 2 Chronicles 22 - 24

❑   I read this passage on   /   /

Prayer	Notes

What God is saying to me

Day 127: 2 Chronicles 25 - 27

❑ I read this passage on / /

Prayer	Notes
	What God is saying to me

Day 128: 2 Chronicles 28 - 30

❏ I read this passage on / /

Prayer	Notes

What God is saying to me

Day 129: 2 Chronicles 31 - 33

❏ I read this passage on / /

Prayer	Notes
	What God is saying to me

Day 130: 2 Chronicles 34 - 36

❑ I read this passage on	/	/

Prayer	Notes
_____	_____
_____	_____
_____	_____
_____	_____
_____	**What God is saying to me**
_____	_____
_____	_____
_____	_____
_____	_____
_____	_____

Day 131: Ezra 1 - 3

❑ I read this passage on / /

Prayer	Notes
	What God is saying to me

It will take **3 days** to finish Ezra.

234 days until you're finished.

Day 132: Ezra 4 - 6

❏ I read this passage on	/	/

Prayer	Notes

What God is saying to me

Day 133: Ezra 7 - 10

❏	I read this passage on	/	/

Prayer	Notes

What God is saying to me

You've finished the book of Ezra. That's **15 of 66** books complete.

232 days until you're finished.

Day 134: Nehemiah 1 - 3

❑ I read this passage on / /

Prayer	Notes
	What God is saying to me

It will take **4 days** to complete your reading of Nehemiah.

231 days until you're finished.

Day 135: Nehemiah 4 - 6

❏	I read this passage on / /

Prayer	Notes
_____	_____
_____	_____
_____	_____
_____	_____
_____	**What God is saying to me**
_____	_____
_____	_____
_____	_____
_____	_____

Halfway through Nehemiah, just like that!

230 days until you're finished.

Day 136: Nehemiah 7 - 9

	I read this passage on	/	/

Prayer	Notes

What God is saying to me

Day 137: Nehemiah 10 - 13

☐ I read this passage on	/	/

Prayer	Notes

What God is saying to me

That was quick! You've finished Nehemiah. That's **16 of 66** books complete.

228 days until you're finished.

Day 138: Esther 1 - 3

❏ I read this passage on / /	
Prayer	**Notes**

What God is saying to me

It will take **3 days** to complete the reading of Esther.

227 days until you're finished.

Day 139: Esther 4 - 6

❏ I read this passage on / /	
Prayer	**Notes**
	What God is saying to me

Day 140: Esther 7 - 10

❑   I read this passage on   /   /

Prayer	Notes

What God is saying to me

And you're finished with the book of Esther. That's **17 of 66** books complete.
225 days until you're finished.

Day 141: Job 1 - 3

❏	I read this passage on / /
Prayer	**Notes**

What God is saying to me

It will take **14 days** to read through Job.

224 days until you're finished.

Day 142: Job 4 - 6

❑ I read this passage on	/ /
Prayer	**Notes**
_____	_____
_____	_____
_____	_____
_____	_____
_____	**What God is saying to me**
_____	_____
_____	_____
_____	_____
_____	_____

Day 143: Job 7 - 9

❏ I read this passage on	/	/

Prayer

Notes

What God is saying to me

Day 144: Job 10 - 12

❑ I read this passage on   /   /

Prayer	Notes
_____	_____
	_____
_____	_____
	_____
_____	_____
	What God is saying to me
_____	_____
_____	_____
_____	_____
_____	_____
_____	_____

Day 145: Job 13 - 15

❏	I read this passage on	/	/

Prayer	Notes

What God is saying to me

Day 146: Job 16 - 18

Prayer	Notes
☐ I read this passage on / /	

Prayer

Notes

_____

_____

_____

_____

_____

_____

_____

_____

What God is saying to me

_____

_____

_____

_____

This is the **40%** complete mark in reading through your Bible.

219 days until you're finished.

Day 147: Job 19 - 21

❏ I read this passage on	/	/

Prayer	Notes

What God is saying to me

Halfway through Job, just like that.
218 days until you're finished.

Day 148: Job 22 - 24

❏ I read this passage on / /	
Prayer	**Notes**
	What God is saying to me

Day 149: Job 25 - 27

| | ❑ | I read this passage on | / | / |

Prayer | **Notes**

_____

_____

_____

_____

_____

What God is saying to me

_____

_____

_____

_____

Day 150: Job 28 - 30

❑ I read this passage on	/ /

Prayer	Notes
	What God is saying to me

Day 151: Job 31 - 33

❏ I read this passage on / /

Prayer	Notes
	What God is saying to me

Day 152: Job 34 - 36

	❏ I read this passage on / /
Prayer	**Notes**
	What God is saying to me

Day 153: Job 37 - 39

❏ I read this passage on / /

Prayer	Notes
	What God is saying to me

Day 154: Job 40 - 42

❑ I read this passage on	/	/

Prayer	Notes
_____	
_____	_____
_____	_____
_____	_____
_____	_____
_____	**What God is saying to me**
_____	_____
_____	_____
_____	_____
_____	_____

You've read through the book of Job. Good stuff, wasn't it? That's **18 of 66** books complete.

211 days until you're finished.

Day 155: Psalm 1 - 5

I read this passage on   /   /

Prayer

Notes

What God is saying to me

You're going to spend a bit of time in Psalms. Don't miss all the fantastic things God says in Psalms. It will take **30 days** to complete Psalms. 210 days until you're finished.

Day 156: Psalm 6 - 10

	I read this passage on / /
Prayer	**Notes**
	What God is saying to me

Day 157: Psalm 11 - 15

❏ I read this passage on	/	/

Prayer	Notes

What God is saying to me

Day 158: Psalm 16 - 20

❏ I read this passage on	/	/

Prayer	Notes
	What God is saying to me

Day 159: Psalm 21 - 25

	I read this passage on / /
Prayer	**Notes**
	What God is saying to me

Day 160: Psalm 26 - 30

❑ I read this passage on	/	/

Prayer	Notes

What God is saying to me

Day 161: Psalm 31 - 35

| | ❏ I read this passage on | / | / |

Prayer	Notes
_____	
	_____
_____	
	_____
_____	
	_____
_____	
	_____
_____	**What God is saying to me**
_____	_____
_____	_____
_____	_____
_____	_____
_____	_____

Day 162: Psalm 36 - 40

❑ I read this passage on	/ /
Prayer	**Notes**

What God is saying to me

Day 163: Psalm 41 - 45

	I read this passage on / /
Prayer	**Notes**
	What God is saying to me

202 days until you're finished.

Day 164: Psalm 46 - 50

❏ I read this passage on / /

Prayer	Notes
	What God is saying to me

Day 165: Psalm 51 - 55

❏ I read this passage on	/	/

Prayer	Notes

What God is saying to me

Day 166: Psalm 56 - 60

Prayer	Notes
❑ I read this passage on / /	

Prayer | **Notes**

What God is saying to me

Day 167: Psalm 61- 65

	I read this passage on / /

Prayer	Notes
_____	_____
_____	_____
_____	_____
_____	_____
_____	**What God is saying to me**
_____	_____
_____	_____
_____	_____
_____	_____

Day 168: Psalm 66 - 70

	❏ I read this passage on / /
Prayer	**Notes**
	What God is saying to me

Day 169: Psalm 71 - 75

☐ I read this passage on / /	
Prayer	**Notes**
	What God is saying to me

This is the **50%** mark through Psalms.

196 days until you're finished.

Day 170: Psalm 76 - 80

❑ I read this passage on	/	/

Prayer	Notes
	What God is saying to me

Day 171: Psalm 81 - 85

❑   I read this passage on   /   /

Prayer	Notes

What God is saying to me

Day 172: Psalm 86 - 90

❏ I read this passage on	/	/
Prayer	**Notes**	

What God is saying to me

Day 173: Psalm 91 - 95

| ❏ I read this passage on | / | / |

Prayer

Notes

What God is saying to me

Day 174: Psalm 96 - 100

❏ I read this passage on / /

Prayer	Notes
_____	
	_____
_____	
	_____
_____	
	_____
_____	
	_____
_____	**What God is saying to me**
_____	_____
_____	_____
_____	_____
_____	_____
_____	_____

Day 175: Psalm 101 - 105

❑ I read this passage on   /   /

Prayer	Notes
_____	_____
_____	_____
_____	_____
_____	_____
_____	**What God is saying to me**
_____	_____
_____	_____
_____	_____
_____	_____

Day 176: Psalm 106 - 110

❏ I read this passage on	/	/

Prayer	Notes

What God is saying to me

Day 177: Psalm 111 - 115

	☐ I read this passage on　　/　　/
Prayer	**Notes**

What God is saying to me

Day 178: Psalm 116 - 120

❏ I read this passage on   /   /

Prayer	Notes
_____	_____
	_____
_____	_____
	_____
_____	
	_____
_____	
	What God is saying to me
_____	
	_____
_____	
	_____
_____	
	_____
_____	
	_____
_____	
	_____

Day 179: Psalm 121 - 125

| | I read this passage on | / | / |

Prayer	Notes

What God is saying to me

188

Day 180: Psalm 126 - 130

❑ I read this passage on	/ /

Prayer	Notes
_____	
	_____
_____	
	_____
_____	
	_____
_____	
	_____
_____	**What God is saying to me**
	_____
_____	
	_____
_____	
	_____
_____	
	_____
_____	

185 days until you're finished.

Day 181: Psalm 131 - 135

	I read this passage on / /
Prayer	**Notes**

What God is saying to me

Day 182: Psalm 136 - 140

❏ I read this passage on	/	/

Prayer	Notes

What God is saying to me

Day 183: Psalm 141 - 145

	❏ I read this passage on / /
Prayer	**Notes**

What God is saying to me

Congratulations! You have now read half the Bible! You're at **50%** complete.

182 days until you're finished.

Day 184: Psalm 146 - 150

❏ I read this passage on   /   /

Prayer	Notes
_____	_____
	_____
_____	_____
_____	_____
_____	**What God is saying to me**
_____	_____
_____	_____
_____	_____
_____	_____

You've just finished Psalms, and it was a blessing, right! That's **19 of 66** books complete.

181 days until you're finished.

Day 185: Proverbs 1 - 3

| | ❏ | I read this passage on | / | / |

Prayer

Notes

_____

_____

_____

_____

_____

_____

_____

_____

_____

_____

What God is saying to me

It will take **10 days** to read through Proverbs.

180 days until you're finished.

Day 186: Proverbs 4 - 6

Prayer	❑ I read this passage on / /
	Notes

What God is saying to me

Day 187: Proverbs 7 - 9

❏ I read this passage on	/	/

Prayer	**Notes**
	What God is saying to me

Day 188: Proverbs 10 - 12

	I read this passage on / /
Prayer	**Notes**

What God is saying to me

Day 189: Proverbs 13 - 15

❏ I read this passage on	/	/

Prayer

Notes

What God is saying to me

You're halfway through Proverbs.

176 days until you're finished.

Day 190: Proverbs 16 - 18

❑ I read this passage on / /	
Prayer	**Notes**

What God is saying to me

Day 191: Proverbs 19 - 21

❑   I read this passage on   /   /

Prayer	Notes

What God is saying to me

Day 192: Proverbs 22 - 24

❏ I read this passage on / /

Prayer	Notes

What God is saying to me

Day 193: Proverbs 25 - 27

❑ I read this passage on   /   /

Prayer	Notes

What God is saying to me

Day 194: Proverbs 28 - 31

	❏ I read this passage on / /
Prayer	**Notes**

What God is saying to me

You've finished Proverbs. That's **20 of 66** books complete.

171 days until you're finished.

Day 195: Ecclesiastes 1 - 3

❑   I read this passage on   /   /

Prayer	Notes

What God is saying to me

It will take **4 days** to read Ecclesiastes.

170 days until you're finished.

Day 196: Ecclesiastes 4 - 6

❏ I read this passage on / /	
Prayer	**Notes**
	What God is saying to me

Halfway through Ecclesiastes already!
169 days until you're finished.

Day 197: Ecclesiastes 7 - 9

❏ I read this passage on	/	/

Prayer	Notes

What God is saying to me

Day 198: Ecclesiastes 10 - 12

❏ I read this passage on   /   /

Prayer	Notes
	What God is saying to me

You have finished Ecclesiastes. That's **21 of 66** books complete.

167 days until you're finished.

Day 199: Song of Songs 1 - 4

❏ I read this passage on ___ / ___ / ___	
Prayer	**Notes**
_____	_____
_____	_____
_____	_____
_____	_____
_____	**What God is saying to me**
_____	_____
_____	_____
_____	_____
_____	_____

It will take only **2 days** to complete Song of Songs.

166 days until you're finished.

Day 200: Song of Songs 5 - 8

❏ I read this passage on   /   /

Prayer	Notes

What God is saying to me

You've finished Song of Songs. That's **22 of 66** books complete.

165 days until you're finished.

Day 201: Isaiah 1- 3

❑ I read this passage on / /

Prayer	Notes

What God is saying to me

It will take <u>22 days</u> to complete Isaiah.

164 days until you're finished.

Day 202: Isaiah 4 - 6

❑ I read this passage on / /

Prayer	Notes
	What God is saying to me

Day 203: Isaiah 7 - 9

❏ I read this passage on / /

Prayer	Notes

What God is saying to me

Day 204: Isaiah 10 - 12

❏ I read this passage on	/	/

Prayer	Notes
	What God is saying to me

Day 205: Isaiah 13 - 15

❏ I read this passage on	/ /
Prayer	**Notes**

What God is saying to me

160 days until you're finished.

214

Day 206: Isaiah 16 - 18

❏ I read this passage on / /

Prayer	Notes
	What God is saying to me

159 days until you're finished.

Day 207: Isaiah 19 - 21

❑   I read this passage on   /   /

Prayer	Notes
	What God is saying to me

Day 208: Isaiah 22 - 24

❏ I read this passage on / /

Prayer	Notes
	What God is saying to me

Day 209: Isaiah 25 - 27

Prayer	Notes
☐ I read this passage on / /	

What God is saying to me

Day 210: Isaiah 28 - 30

❑　　I read this passage on 　　　/　　　　/	

Prayer	Notes
	What God is saying to me

Day 211: Isaiah 31 - 33

	I read this passage on / /
Prayer	**Notes**

What God is saying to me

Today marks the halfway point of reading through Isaiah.

154 days until you're finished.

220

Day 212: Isaiah 34 - 36

Prayer	Notes

☐ I read this passage on   /   /

What God is saying to me

Day 213: Isaiah 37 - 39

❏ I read this passage on	/ /

Prayer	Notes
_____	
	_____
_____	
	_____
_____	
	_____
_____	
	_____
_____	**What God is saying to me**
_____	_____
_____	_____
_____	_____
_____	_____
_____	_____

Day 214: Isaiah 40 - 42

	❏ I read this passage on / /
Prayer	**Notes**
	What God is saying to me

Day 215: Isaiah 43 - 45

❏　　I read this passage on	/　　　　/

Prayer	Notes

What God is saying to me

Day 216: Isaiah 46 - 48

❏ I read this passage on / /

Prayer	Notes
	What God is saying to me

Day 217: Isaiah 49 - 51

❏ I read this passage on / /

Prayer	Notes
	What God is saying to me

Day 218: Isaiah 52 - 54

❏ I read this passage on	/ /

Prayer	Notes

What God is saying to me

Day 219: Isaiah 55 - 57

| ❏ | I read this passage on | / | / |

Prayer	Notes
	What God is saying to me

Day 220: Isaiah 58 - 60

❏   I read this passage on   /   /

Prayer	Notes

What God is saying to me

Day 221: Isaiah 61 - 63

❏   I read this passage on   /   /

Prayer	Notes
	What God is saying to me

Day 222: Isaiah 64 - 66

❏ I read this passage on / /	
Prayer	**Notes**
	What God is saying to me

You've completed Isaiah. That's **23 of 66** books complete.

143 days until you're finished.

Day 223: Jeremiah 1 - 3

❑ I read this passage on / /	
Prayer	**Notes**
	What God is saying to me

It will take **17 days** to complete Jeremiah.

142 days until you're finished.

Day 224: Jeremiah 4 - 6

❏ I read this passage on / /	
Prayer	**Notes**
_____	_____
	_____
_____	_____
	_____
_____	_____
	_____
_____	
	What God is saying to me
_____	
	_____
_____	
	_____
_____	
	_____
_____	
	_____
_____	

Day 225: Jeremiah 7 - 9

❏ I read this passage on / /

Prayer	Notes
	What God is saying to me

Day 226: Jeremiah 10 - 12

	❏ I read this passage on / /
Prayer	**Notes**
	What God is saying to me

Day 227: Jeremiah 13 - 15

❏　　I read this passage on　　　/　　　　/	
Prayer	**Notes**
	What God is saying to me

Day 228: Jeremiah 16 - 18

❏ I read this passage on / /	
Prayer	**Notes**
	What God is saying to me

Day 229: Jeremiah 19 - 21

❏ I read this passage on / /

Prayer	Notes
	What God is saying to me

Day 230: Jeremiah 22 - 24

❏ I read this passage on	/	/

Prayer	Notes

What God is saying to me

Day 231: Jeremiah 25 - 27

❑ I read this passage on	/	/

Prayer

Notes

What God is saying to me

You're now over halfway through Jeremiah.

134 days until you're finished.

text

240

Day 232: Jeremiah 28 - 30

❑ I read this passage on / /

Prayer	Notes
_____	_____
_____	_____
_____	_____
_____	_____
_____	**What God is saying to me**
_____	_____
_____	_____
_____	_____
_____	_____

Day 233: Jeremiah 31 - 33

	❏ I read this passage on / /
Prayer	**Notes**
	What God is saying to me

Day 234: Jeremiah 34 - 36

❏ I read this passage on	/ /

Prayer	Notes

What God is saying to me

Day 235: Jeremiah 37 - 39

❑ I read this passage on / /

Prayer	Notes
	What God is saying to me

130 days until you're finished.

Day 236: Jeremiah 40 - 42

Prayer	Notes
❑ I read this passage on / /	

Prayer

Notes

What God is saying to me

Day 237: Jeremiah 43 - 45

❑ I read this passage on / /

Prayer	Notes
	What God is saying to me

Day 238: Jeremiah 46 - 48

❑ I read this passage on / /	
Prayer	**Notes**
	What God is saying to me

127 days until you're finished.

Day 239: Jeremiah 49 - 52

❏ I read this passage on	/ /

Prayer	Notes

What God is saying to me

Moving on! That completes Jeremiah. That's **24 of 66** books complete.

126 days until you're finished.

Day 240: Lamentations 1 - 3

❏ I read this passage on / /	

Prayer	Notes
_____	_____
_____	_____
_____	_____
_____	_____

What God is saying to me

_____	_____
_____	_____
_____	_____
_____	_____

2 short days and you'll finish Lamentations.

125 days until you're finished.

Day 241: Lamentations 4 - 5

☐ I read this passage on	/	/

Prayer	Notes
_____	_____
_____	_____
_____	_____
_____	_____
_____	_____
_____	**What God is saying to me**
_____	_____
_____	_____
_____	_____
_____	_____
_____	_____

That's it. You've finished Lamentations. That's __25 of 66__ books complete.

124 days until you're finished.

Day 242: Ezekiel 1 - 3

❏ I read this passage on	/	/

Prayer	Notes
	What God is saying to me

It will take **15 days** to complete Ezekiel.

123 days until you're finished.

Day 243: Ezekiel 4 - 6

❏   I read this passage on   /   /

Prayer	Notes
_____	
	_____
_____	
	_____
_____	
	_____
_____	
_____	**What God is saying to me**
_____	_____
_____	_____
_____	_____
_____	_____
_____	_____

Day 244: Ezekiel 7 - 9

| ❏ I read this passage on | / | / |

Prayer	Notes
	What God is saying to me

Day 245: Ezekiel 10 - 12

❑ I read this passage on / /	
Prayer	**Notes**
	What God is saying to me

Day 246: Ezekiel 13 - 15

❏ I read this passage on	/	/

Prayer	Notes
	What God is saying to me

Day 247: Ezekiel 16 - 18

Prayer	Notes

☐   I read this passage on   /   /

What God is saying to me

Day 248: Ezekiel 19 - 21

Prayer	Notes

□ I read this passage on   /   /

What God is saying to me

Day 249: Ezekiel 22 - 24

☐ I read this passage on / /

Prayer	Notes
	What God is saying to me

Today puts you a bit over halfway through Ezekiel.

116 days until you're finished.

Day 250: Ezekiel 25 - 27

❏ I read this passage on / /	

Prayer	Notes
_____	_____
	_____
_____	
	_____
_____	
	_____
_____	
	_____
_____	**What God is saying to me**
	_____
_____	
	_____
_____	
	_____
_____	
	_____
_____	

Day 251: Ezekiel 28 - 30

❏ I read this passage on / /

Prayer	Notes
	What God is saying to me

Day 252: Ezekiel 31 - 33

❏ I read this passage on / /	
Prayer	**Notes**
	What God is saying to me

Day 253: Ezekiel 34 - 36

❏ I read this passage on	/	/

Prayer	Notes

What God is saying to me

Day 254: Ezekiel 37 - 40

❏ I read this passage on	/	/

Prayer	Notes
_____	_____
	_____
_____	
	_____
_____	
	_____
_____	
_____	**What God is saying to me**
	_____
_____	
	_____
_____	
	_____
_____	
	_____
_____	

Day 255: Ezekiel 41 - 44

	I read this passage on	/	/

Prayer	Notes

What God is saying to me

Day 256: Ezekiel 45 - 48

❑ I read this passage on / /	
Prayer	**Notes**
_____	_____
	_____
_____	
	_____
_____	_____
_____	
	What God is saying to me
_____	
	_____
_____	
	_____
_____	_____
_____	_____
_____	_____

Look. You've finished reading **70%** of the Bible!

You've also finished Ezekiel. That's **26 of 66** books complete. 109 days until you're finished.

Day 257: Daniel 1 - 3

❏ I read this passage on / /		

Prayer	Notes

What God is saying to me

It will take **4 days** to complete Daniel.

108 days until you're finished.

Day 258: Daniel 4 - 6

❏	I read this passage on	/	/

Prayer	Notes
_____	_____
	_____
_____	_____
	_____
_____	
	_____
_____	
_____	**What God is saying to me**
	_____
_____	
	_____
_____	
	_____
_____	
	_____
_____	
	_____

You're already 50% through Daniel.

107 days until you're finished.

Day 259: Daniel 7 - 9

❑ I read this passage on / /

Prayer	Notes

What God is saying to me

Day 260: Daniel 10 - 12

☐	I read this passage on / /
Prayer	**Notes**
	What God is saying to me

You're done with Daniel. That's **27 of 66** books complete.

105 days until you're finished.

Day 261: Hosea 1 - 3

❑ I read this passage on	/	/

Prayer	Notes
	What God is saying to me

Day 262: Hosea 4 - 6

❏ I read this passage on / /	

Prayer	Notes
	What God is saying to me

Halfway through Hosea already!
103 days until you're finished.

Day 263: Hosea 7 - 10

Prayer	Notes

☐ I read this passage on   /   /

What God is saying to me

272

Day 264: Hosea 11 - 14

	❑ I read this passage on / /
Prayer	**Notes**

What God is saying to me

You've finished Hosea. That's **28 of 66** books complete.
101 days until you're finished.

Day 265: Joel 1 - 3

❏   I read this passage on   /   /

Prayer	Notes

What God is saying to me

One day and done with Joel. That's **29 of 66** books complete.

100 days until you're finished.

Day 266: Amos 1- 3

❏ I read this passage on / /

Prayer	Notes
_____	_____
_____	_____
_____	_____
_____	_____
_____	**What God is saying to me**
_____	_____
_____	_____
_____	_____
_____	_____

It will take **3 days** to read Amos.

99 days until you're finished.

Day 267: Amos 4 - 6

| ❑ | I read this passage on | / | / |

Prayer	Notes

What God is saying to me

Day 268: Amos 7 - 9

❏ I read this passage on	/ /

Prayer	Notes

What God is saying to me

And Amos is done. That's **30 of 66** books complete.

97 days until you're finished.

Day 269: Obadiah

Prayer	Notes
☐ I read this passage on / /	

Prayer

Notes

_____

_____

_____

_____

_____

_____

_____

What God is saying to me

_____

_____

_____

_____

One and done with Obadiah. That's **31 of 66** books complete.

96 days until you're finished.

278

Day 270: Jonah 1 - 4

	❑ I read this passage on　　　/　　　/
Prayer	**Notes**

What God is saying to me

The books will go quickly now. **Done** with Jonah. That's **32 of 66** books complete.
95 days until you're finished.

Day 271: Micah 1 - 3

| | ❏ | I read this passage on | / | / |

Prayer	Notes
	What God is saying to me

It will take **2 days** to complete Micah.

94 days until you're finished.

Day 272: Micah 4 - 7

| | ❑ I read this passage on | / | / |

Prayer	Notes
_____	_____
	_____
_____	_____
	_____
_____	_____
	_____
_____	**What God is saying to me**
	_____
_____	_____
	_____
_____	_____
	_____
_____	_____
	_____

Micah is done. That's **33 of 66** books complete.

93 days until you're finished.

Day 273: Nahum 1 - 3

☐ I read this passage on / /

Prayer	Notes
_____	_____
_____	_____
_____	_____
_____	_____
_____	**What God is saying to me**
_____	_____
_____	_____
_____	_____
_____	_____
_____	_____

Quick read and **done** with Nahum. That's **34 of 66** books complete.

92 days until you're finished.

Day 274: Habakkuk 1 - 3

	❏ I read this passage on / /
Prayer	**Notes**
	What God is saying to me

You're getting closer. You are __75%__ complete in your reading through the Bible.

That's it for Habakkuk, too. That's **35 of 66** books complete. 91 days until you're finished.

Day 275: Zephaniah 1 - 3

❏	I read this passage on	/	/

Prayer	Notes

What God is saying to me

You're **done** with Zephaniah. That's **36 of 66** books complete.

90 days until you're finished.

Day 276: Haggai 1 - 2

❏ I read this passage on / /

Prayer	Notes
_____	
	_____
_____	
	_____
_____	
	_____
_____	
	_____
_____	**What God is saying to me**
_____	_____
_____	_____
_____	_____
_____	_____

Haggai is finished. That's **37 of 66** books complete.

89 days until you're finished.

Day 277: Zechariah 1 - 3

❏ I read this passage on	/ /

Prayer	Notes

What God is saying to me

It will take **4 days** to finish Zechariah.

88 days until you're finished.

Day 278: Zechariah 4 - 6

❏ I read this passage on	/ /

Prayer	Notes
	What God is saying to me

Halfway through Zechariah.

87 days until you're finished.

Day 279: Zechariah 7 - 10

❏	I read this passage on / /

Prayer	Notes

What God is saying to me

288

Day 280: Zechariah 11 - 14

❑ I read this passage on / /	
Prayer	**Notes**
_____	_____
_____	_____
_____	_____
_____	_____
_____	**What God is saying to me**
_____	_____
_____	_____
_____	_____
_____	_____

You're finished with Zechariah. That's **38 of 66** books complete.

85 days until you're finished.

Day 281: Malachi 1 - 2

❏   I read this passage on   /   /

Prayer	Notes

What God is saying to me

It will take **2 days** to complete Malachi.

84 days until you're finished.

290

Day 282: Malachi 3 - 4

| | ❏ | I read this passage on | / | / |

Prayer	Notes
	What God is saying to me

You've finished Malachi. **And you've finished the Old Testament today!**

You'll move into the New Testament next. That's **39 of 66** books complete. 83 days until you're finished.

Day 283: Matthew 1 - 3

❑ I read this passage on   /   /

Prayer	Notes

What God is saying to me

Welcome to the New Testament! It will take **9 days** to complete Matthew.

82 days until you're finished.

Day 284: Matthew 4 - 6

❏   I read this passage on   /   /

Prayer	Notes

What God is saying to me

Day 285: Matthew 7 - 9

❏ I read this passage on / /

Prayer	Notes
	What God is saying to me

Day 286: Matthew 10 -12

❏ I read this passage on / /	
Prayer	**Notes**
	What God is saying to me

79 days until you're finished.

Day 287: Matthew 13 - 15

| ☐ I read this passage on | / | / |

Prayer

Notes

What God is saying to me

You're over halfway through Matthew today.

78 days until you're finished.

Day 288: Matthew 16 - 18

❑	I read this passage on	/ /

Prayer	Notes

What God is saying to me

Day 289: Matthew 19 - 21

❑ I read this passage on   /   /

Prayer	Notes

What God is saying to me

Day 290: Matthew 22 - 24

❏ I read this passage on / /	
Prayer	**Notes**
_____	_____
_____	_____
_____	_____
_____	_____
_____	**What God is saying to me**
_____	_____
_____	_____
_____	_____
_____	_____

Day 291: Matthew 25 - 28

| | ❏ | I read this passage on | / | / |

Prayer

Notes

What God is saying to me

You're through Matthew. That's **40 of 66** books complete.

74 days until you're finished.

Day 292: Mark 1 - 3

❏ I read this passage on / /

Prayer	Notes
	What God is saying to me

As you finish today's reading you have reached **80%** completion.

It will take **5 days** to complete Mark. 73 days until you're finished.

Day 293: Mark 4 - 6

❏ I read this passage on / /

Prayer	Notes

What God is saying to me

Day 294: Mark 7 - 9

☐ I read this passage on / /

Prayer	Notes
	What God is saying to me

You're a bit over halfway through Mark.

71 days until you're finished.

Day 295: Mark 10 - 12

☐	I read this passage on	/	/

Prayer	Notes

What God is saying to me

Day 296: Mark 13 - 16

❏ I read this passage on	/	/

Prayer	Notes

What God is saying to me

You've finished Mark. That's **41 of 66** books complete.

69 days until you're finished.

Day 297: Luke 1 - 3

❑ I read this passage on / /	
Prayer	**Notes**
	What God is saying to me

It will take **8 days** to read through Luke.

68 days until you're finished.

Day 298: Luke 4 - 6

	❏ I read this passage on / /
Prayer	**Notes**

What God is saying to me

Day 299: Luke 7 - 9

☐ I read this passage on	/	/

Prayer	Notes

What God is saying to me

Day 300: Luke 10 - 12

❏ I read this passage on	/	/

Prayer	Notes
_____	_____
_____	_____
_____	_____
_____	_____
_____	**What God is saying to me**
_____	_____
_____	_____
_____	_____
_____	_____

Day 301: Luke 13 - 15

❏ I read this passage on / /	

Prayer	Notes
	What God is saying to me

Day 302: Luke 16 - 18

❏ I read this passage on	/	/

Prayer	Notes

What God is saying to me

Day 303: Luke 19 - 21

❑ I read this passage on   /   /

Prayer	Notes
	What God is saying to me

Day 304: Luke 22 - 24

❑ I read this passage on	/	/

Prayer	Notes
_____	
	_____
_____	
	_____
_____	
	_____
_____	
	_____
_____	**What God is saying to me**
_____	_____
_____	_____
_____	_____
_____	_____

That closes out Luke and that's **42 of 66** books complete.

61 days until you're finished.

Day 305: John 1 - 3

| ❑ I read this passage on | / | / |

Prayer

Notes

What God is saying to me

It will take **7 days** to complete John.

60 days until you're finished.

Day 306: John 4 - 6

❏ I read this passage on / /	
Prayer	**Notes**
_____	
	_____
_____	
	_____
_____	
	_____
_____	
	_____
_____	**What God is saying to me**
_____	_____
_____	_____
_____	_____
_____	_____
_____	_____

Day 307: John 7 - 9

❑ I read this passage on / /	
Prayer	**Notes**
_____	_____
_____	_____
_____	_____
_____	_____
_____	**What God is saying to me**
_____	_____
_____	_____
_____	_____
_____	_____

58 days until you're finished.

Day 308: John 10 - 12

	☐ I read this passage on / /

Prayer	Notes
	What God is saying to me

You're now over halfway through John.

57 days until you're finished.

Day 309: John 13 - 15

☐ I read this passage on	/	/

Prayer	Notes

What God is saying to me

Day 310: John 16 - 18

❑	I read this passage on	/ /

Prayer	Notes
_____	_____
_____	_____
_____	_____
_____	_____
	_____
_____	**What God is saying to me**
_____	_____
_____	_____
_____	_____
_____	_____
_____	_____

Day 311: John 19 - 21

❑　　I read this passage on　　　/　　　/	
Prayer	**Notes**
	What God is saying to me

You've finished John and the Gospels. That's **43 of 66** books complete.

54 days until you're finished.

Day 312: Acts 1 - 3

❏ I read this passage on / /	
Prayer	**Notes**

What God is saying to me

It will take **9 days** to finish Acts.

53 days until you're finished.

Day 313: Acts 4 - 6

| ☐ | I read this passage on | / | / |

Prayer	Notes
	What God is saying to me

Day 314: Acts 7 - 9

❏ I read this passage on	/	/

Prayer	Notes

What God is saying to me

Day 315: Acts 10 - 12

❑ I read this passage on / /	
Prayer	Notes
	What God is saying to me

Day 316: Acts 13 - 15

❏ I read this passage on	/	/

Prayer	Notes

What God is saying to me

Day 317: Acts 16 - 18

	I read this passage on / /
Prayer	**Notes**

What God is saying to me

Day 318: Acts 19 - 21

❑   I read this passage on   /   /

Prayer	Notes

What God is saying to me

Day 319: Acts 22 - 24

❑ I read this passage on / /

Prayer	Notes
	What God is saying to me

Day 320: Acts 25 - 28

| ❏ | I read this passage on | / | / |

Prayer	Notes

What God is saying to me

You've made it through Acts. That's **44 of 66** books complete.

45 days until you're finished.

Day 321: Romans 1 - 3

	I read this passage on / /
Prayer	**Notes**

What God is saying to me

It will take **5 days** to complete Romans.

44 days until you're finished.

Day 322: Romans 4 - 6

	❏ I read this passage on / /
Prayer	**Notes**
	What God is saying to me

Day 323: Romans 7 - 9

❏	I read this passage on	/ /

Prayer	Notes

What God is saying to me

Just a bit past halfway through Romans.

42 days until you're finished.

Day 324: Romans 10 - 12

❏ I read this passage on / /

Prayer	Notes
	What God is saying to me

Day 325: Romans 13 - 16

❏ I read this passage on	/ /

Prayer	Notes
	What God is saying to me

You've finished the wonderful book of Romans. That's **45 of 66** books complete.

40 days until you're finished.

Day 326: 1 Corinthians 1 - 3

❏ I read this passage on   /   /

Prayer	Notes

What God is saying to me

It will take **5 days** to complete 1 Corinthians.

39 days until you're finished.

Day 327: 1 Corinthians 4 - 6

☐	I read this passage on	/	/

Prayer	Notes

What God is saying to me

Day 328: 1 Corinthians 7 - 9

❑　　　I read this passage on　　　　/　　　　　/	
Prayer	**Notes**
_____	_____
_____	_____
_____	_____
_____	_____
_____	**What God is saying to me**
_____	_____
_____	_____
_____	_____
_____	_____

You're past the halfway mark in 1 Corinthians.

37 days until you're finished.

X

Day 329: 1 Corinthians 10 - 12

❑ I read this passage on   /   /

Prayer

Notes

What God is saying to me

Almost there! This is the **90%** mark in completing the Bible.

36 days until you're finished.

Day 330: 1 Corinthians 13 - 16

❏ I read this passage on	/	/

Prayer	Notes

What God is saying to me

You're done with 1 Corinthians. That's **46 of 66** books complete.

35 days until you're finished.

Day 331: 2 Corinthians 1 - 3

❑ I read this passage on / /

Prayer	Notes
_____	_____
_____	_____
_____	_____
_____	_____
_____	**What God is saying to me**
_____	_____
_____	_____
_____	_____
_____	_____

It will take **4 days** to finish 2 Corinthians.

34 days until you're finished.

Day 332: 2 Corinthians 4 - 6

	❏ I read this passage on / /
Prayer	**Notes**
_____	_____
_____	_____
_____	_____
_____	_____
_____	**What God is saying to me**
_____	_____
_____	_____
_____	_____
_____	_____

Day 333: 2 Corinthians 7 - 9

❑ I read this passage on   /   /

Prayer	Notes

What God is saying to me

Day 334: 2 Corinthians 10 - 13

❑ I read this passage on	/ /

Prayer	Notes
_____	_____
_____	_____
_____	_____
_____	_____
_____	**What God is saying to me**
_____	_____
_____	_____
_____	_____
_____	_____

You're done with 2 Corinthians. That's **47 of 66** books complete.

31 days until you're finished.

Day 335: Galatians 1 - 3

❏   I read this passage on   /   /

Prayer	Notes
	What God is saying to me

Things will pick up in pace now. It will take **2 days** to finish Galatians.

30 days until you're finished.

Day 336: Galatians 4 - 6

Prayer	Notes
❑ I read this passage on / /	

What God is saying to me

You've finished Galatians. That's **48 of 66** books complete.

29 days until you're finished.

Day 337: Ephesians 1 - 3

Prayer	Notes
❏ I read this passage on / /	

Prayer

Notes

What God is saying to me

Day 338: Ephesians 4 - 6

❏ I read this passage on	/	/

Prayer	Notes
_____	_____
_____	_____
_____	_____
_____	_____
_____	**What God is saying to me**
_____	_____
_____	_____
_____	_____
_____	_____

That completes Ephesians and that also completes **49 of 66** books.

27 days until you're finished.

Day 339: Philippians 1 - 4

❏ I read this passage on   /   /

Prayer	Notes

What God is saying to me

That's it for Philippians. That's **50 of 66** books complete.

26 days until you're finished.

Day 340: Colossians 1 - 4

❏ I read this passage on	/	/

Prayer	Notes

What God is saying to me

Colossians is finished. That's **51 of 66** books complete.

25 days until you're finished.

Day 341: 1 Thessalonians 1 - 5

	❏	I read this passage on	/	/

Prayer	Notes

What God is saying to me

You're finished with 1 Thessalonians. That's <u>**52 of 66**</u> books complete.

24 days until you're finished.

Day 342: 2 Thessalonians 1 - 3

❑ I read this passage on / /

Prayer	Notes
_____	
	_____
_____	
	_____
_____	
	_____
_____	
	_____
_____	**What God is saying to me**
_____	_____
	_____
_____	
	_____
_____	
	_____
_____	
	_____

And that completes 2 Thessalonians, and that's **53 of 66** books complete.

23 days until you're finished.

Day 343: 1 Timothy 1 - 3

❑   I read this passage on   /   /

Prayer	Notes

What God is saying to me

It will take **2 days** to complete 1 Timothy.

22 days until you're finished.

Day 344: 1 Timothy 4 - 6

| | ❏ | I read this passage on | / | / |

Prayer	Notes
_____	
	_____
_____	
	_____
_____	
	_____
_____	
	_____
_____	**What God is saying to me**
_____	_____
_____	_____
_____	_____
_____	_____

You've completed 1 Timothy and **54 of 66** books.

21 days until you're finished.

353

Day 345: 2 Timothy 1 - 4

❑ I read this passage on   /   /

Prayer

Notes

What God is saying to me

That finishes 2 Timothy. That's **55 of 66** books complete.

20 days until you're finished.

354

Day 346: Titus 1 - 3

Prayer	Notes

❏   I read this passage on   /   /

What God is saying to me

You've finished Titus. That's **56 of 66** books complete.

19 days until you're finished.

Day 347: Philemon

❏ I read this passage on / /	

Prayer	Notes
_____	_____
_____	_____
_____	_____
_____	_____
_____	**What God is saying to me**
_____	_____
_____	_____
_____	_____
_____	_____

Short day! You've finished Philemon. That's **57 of 66** books complete.

18 days until you're finished.

Day 348: Hebrews 1 - 3

	☐ I read this passage on / /
Prayer	**Notes**
_____	_____
_____	_____
_____	_____
_____	_____
_____	**What God is saying to me**
_____	_____
_____	_____
_____	_____
_____	_____

It will take **4 days** to finish Hebrews.

17 days until you're finished.

Day 349: Hebrews 4 - 6

❏ I read this passage on / /	
Prayer	**Notes**

What God is saying to me

Halfway done with Hebrews.

16 days until you're finished.

358

Day 350: Hebrews 7 - 9

❏   I read this passage on   /   /

Prayer	Notes

What God is saying to me

15 days until you're finished.

Day 351: Hebrews 10 - 13

❑ I read this passage on	/	/

Prayer	Notes
_____	
	_____
_____	
	_____
_____	
	_____
_____	
	_____
_____	**What God is saying to me**
_____	_____
_____	_____
_____	_____
_____	_____
_____	_____

You're done with Hebrews. That's **58 of 66** books complete.

14 days until you're finished.

Day 352: James 1- 3

❑ I read this passage on / /	
Prayer	**Notes**
_____	_____
_____	_____
_____	_____
_____	_____
_____	**What God is saying to me**
_____	_____
_____	_____
_____	_____
_____	_____
_____	_____

It will take **2 days** to finish James.

13 days until you're finished.

Day 353: James 4 - 5

❏ I read this passage on / /	

Prayer	Notes
_____	_____
_____	_____
_____	_____
_____	_____
_____	**What God is saying to me**
_____	_____
_____	_____
_____	_____
_____	_____

Done with James. That's **59 of 66** books complete.

12 days until you're finished.

Day 354: 1 Peter 1 - 5

❑ I read this passage on / /	
Prayer	**Notes**
_____	_____
_____	_____
_____	_____
_____	_____
_____	**What God is saying to me**
_____	_____
_____	_____
_____	_____
_____	_____
_____	_____

You have finished 1 Peter and that completes **60 of 66** books.

11 days until you're finished.

Day 355: 2 Peter 1 - 3

❏ I read this passage on / /	
Prayer	**Notes**

What God is saying to me

2 Peter is finished. That completes **61 of 66** books.

10 days until you're finished.

Day 356: 1 John 1 - 3

	I read this passage on / /

Prayer	Notes
_____	_____
_____	_____
_____	_____
_____	_____
_____	**What God is saying to me**
_____	_____
_____	_____
_____	_____
_____	_____
_____	_____

It will take **2 days** to complete 1 John.

9 days until you're finished.

Day 357: 1 John 4 - 5

Prayer	Notes

❏   I read this passage on   /   /

Prayer

Notes

What God is saying to me

That's all for 1 John. That completes **62 of 66** books.

8 days until you're finished.

Day 358: 2 John, 3 John and Jude

❏ I read this passage on   /   /

Prayer	Notes

What God is saying to me

3 books in 1 day! You've finished 1 John, 2 John, and Jude. You've now completed **65 of 66** books.

7 days until you're finished.

Day 359: Revelation 1 - 3

	I read this passage on / /

Prayer	Notes
	What God is saying to me

You've reached the last book of the Bible! It will take **7 days** to complete Revelation.

6 days until you're finished.

Day 360: Revelation 4 - 6

☐ I read this passage on / /

Prayer	Notes
_____	
	_____
_____	
	_____
_____	
	_____
_____	
	_____
_____	**What God is saying to me**
_____	_____
_____	_____
_____	_____
_____	_____

Day 361: Revelation 7 - 9

	I read this passage on / /
Prayer	**Notes**
_____	_____
_____	_____
_____	_____
_____	_____
_____	**What God is saying to me**
_____	_____
_____	_____
_____	_____
_____	_____

4 days until you're finished.

Day 362: Revelation 10 - 12

	I read this passage on / /

Prayer	Notes
_____	_____
_____	_____
_____	_____
_____	_____
_____	**What God is saying to me**
_____	_____
_____	_____
_____	_____
_____	_____

You're over halfway through Revelation. The end is in sight!

3 days until you're finished.

Day 363: Revelation 13 - 15

	I read this passage on / /

Prayer	Notes
	What God is saying to me

2 days until you're finished.

Day 364: Revelation 16 - 18

❑ I read this passage on / /	
Prayer	**Notes**
_____	_____
_____	_____
_____	_____
_____	_____
_____	**What God is saying to me**
_____	_____
_____	_____
_____	_____
_____	_____
_____	_____

Day 365: Revelation 19 - 22

❏ I read this passage on / /	
Prayer	**Notes**
_____	_____
_____	_____
_____	_____
_____	_____
_____	**What God is saying to me**
_____	_____
_____	_____
_____	_____
_____	_____

YOU'RE DONE! Fireworks! Bells! Whistles! Fantastic! Turn the page for what's next.

Congratulations!

You now have an accomplishment many have started but many less have finished. Reading the Bible completely through is something you will always remember. You have read, word-for-word, the whole counsel of the Word of God. You've completed an epic journey you share with those who've also walked this road over the last centuries. Good job.

What Do I Do Now?

There's several things you should do, now that you've reached your goal.

- Take some time to go back through your journal. Let those memories you built with God over the last year be rekindled and refreshed.
- Flip through your journal and note the prayers you've written over the past year. Do you see where God answered your prayers? Do you see how your prayers might have changed through the year? Are there still prayers you need to keep praying?
- Spend some time reading through the notes you recorded as you read. Are there some things you may have forgotten and need to do? What were some of the particularly meaningful things you recorded?
- Take your time reading through the *What God is Saying to Me?* Sections on each page. Are there some things you still need to do as a result of God speaking to you? Can you see how God might have spoke to you in ways that changed who you are and where you're going?
- Pray and thank God for helping you persevere in your reading. Thank Him for everything He did as you read. Ask Him to give you the strength and ability to do and become all He wants you to be.

- Start again! You've developed a habit that will serve you well throughout your life. Don't stop now. Start over. Grab another one of these journals and begin the journey again!

Father, we thank you for the wonderful, living Word that you've given us. Thank you for speaking to us through it. Thank you for drawing near to us as we drew near to you. And thank you for Jesus and what He's done for us. Thank you for the redemption we've received from you and the pages we've read that point to You and your great salvation. Amen.

About the Author

Rob Westbrook became a follower of Jesus Christ at the later age of thirty. Called into the preaching ministry at thirty-two, Rob attended New Orleans Baptist Theological Seminary, earning a Bachelors of Arts degree in Pastoral Ministry. He later earned forty-six hours toward a Masters of Divinity degree.

Rob became pastor of his first church, Hebron Baptist Church, in Amite County, Mississippi, in 1998, while attending seminary. By 2002 the time commitments to both seminary and the church became strained, and Rob chose to leave seminary behind for the church. Around 2005, God began preparing him for planting a new church. He left his first church pastorate in 2006 to become a church planter in his hometown of Amory, Mississippi. LifePointe Church had its first service in January 2008. Rob currently serves there, at LifePointe Church.
Rob has been married to Teresa for almost 23 years. He and Teresa have one daughter, Lauren, who is engaged to Brandon Britt. They will be married in March 2013.

Rob also has published the **Sermon Outlines for Busy Pastors** series, as well as other books relating to the church.

You can find Rob at his website: **http://www.robwestbrook.com**
You can find Rob's books at: **http://busypastorsermons.com**
Follow him on Twitter: **http://twitter.com/robwestbrook**
Find him on Facebook: **http://www.facebook.com/robwestbrook**